A Book of

DR R BRASCH

GOOD ADVICE

Angus&Robertson
An imprint of HarperCollins*Publishers*

Contents

Introduction 1

Opening Lines 3

Don't Underestimate People's Intelligence 5

Unexpected Finds 6

A Lesson Learnt from Worms 8

Avoid Common Errors 9

Don't be All-wise 11

Don't Think it is Just You 12

Do You Know Where You Are Going? 13

Make Every Day Count 14

Don't be Negative 15

Disarming Aggression 16

In Search of Praise 18

Speaking One's Mind 19

The Curse of Jealousy 20

What a Smile Can Do 22

Preserving the Family Unit 24

I am not a Tree 26

Wrong Legacies 28

The Worst Computer Virus 29

We are not Worlds Apart 30

On Being Tolerant 32

Come to the Point 34

Table Talk 35

When Time Seems to Drag 36

Watching the Clock 37

Be on Time 38

A Useful Reminder 40

Self-destructing Problems 42

The Friendship Quilt 44

The Lace Handkerchief 46

A Confusion of Values 47

Don't be a Successful Failure 48

A Built-in Safety Valve 50

Do What You Can — When You Can 51

I've Had It! 52

What One Person Can Do 54

Introduction

A man stopped me in the street. Most probably I would not remember him, he said, but our chance encounter meant so much to him. For a long time he had intended to phone or write to thank me.

As he had assumed, I did not recognise him. He was middle-aged and seemed very sincere and I felt that he genuinely meant what he was saying. Naturally, I wondered what it was that I had done to earn his gratitude.

Without any prompting on my part, he gave the explanation. Now managing a large branch of a bank, he was convinced that he owed his position to me, which mystified me even more.

He told me how, early on in his career, when he was working as a teller, I used to be one of his customers. We had become friendly and had had many a chat. One day, whilst he was not busy, we had started to talk about work ethics and communication. In the course of conversation I had related to him some principles which I had adopted early on in life. I had made it my practice never to be too busy for people who wanted to speak to me. Moreover, no matter who they were and how crowded my schedule, I never let them feel that I was pressed for time. Making them welcome, I wanted them to know that for them (whatever their problem) I had all the time in the world. Also, I never asked a caller, 'What do you want?' Instead, I inquired, 'What can I do for you?'

The man continued, telling me that my practice had immediately caught his imagination, in fact, it had changed his entire lifestyle. On the very day of our talk he had decided to apply my ways, doing so not as a gimmick — shams are always short-lived — but genuinely. 'It did not take long to come to the notice of my superiors,' he continued, 'and I rapidly advanced on the ladder of promotion.' At the time of our meeting he had been a bank manager for many years.

This is merely one example of what this book is all about. It is meant to share with you some of my observations and philosophies of life. I hope that it might prove useful to you in your own life. If nothing else, it may provide some food for thought.

R. Brasch

Opening Lines

When browsing in a bookstore, the opening lines of a book may whet your appetite to buy it or make you put it back on the shelf. The way in which a speaker commences a talk may immediately capture the audience's attention or cause it to lose interest straightaway and, metaphorically, close their ears, if not their eyes.

Equally effective is the manner in which you approach a person or problem — anything. A good start promises the likelihood of a good ending.

On whatever you embark, do so in the very manner in which you want to carry on. This rule should be applied to every kind of life situation. How you act on first meeting a person determines the follow-up. Indifference may result in rejection. A show of genuine interest, on the other hand, will lead to a fruitful association. Concern displayed and a polite introduction, possibly accompanied by a genuine smile may pay unexpected dividends. The opening lines, as it were, are your signature tune. They not only anticipate but influence all that is to come.

Life is full of new beginnings. There is a great thrill in starting anything new: the first day at school or college, or the launching of a new project, career or enterprise. Above all, vitally important is the way in which you begin a relationship. Anything commenced half-heartedly, with doubts, insincerely or in a listless spirit is bound to fail. To begin enthusiastically, however, ensures 'wellbeing' and 'well-doing'.

At one time, people anxiously observed with which foot they entered a home. To put the wrong foot first, they felt, augured bad luck. This explains the early existence of 'footmen', their very name. Taking up position at the threshold of the homes of English nobility, it was their specific duty to watch out and make sure that, on entering, guests and visitors would put their right foot first. Certainly, the custom was a mere superstition. It is not a superstition, however, but wisdom, at all times to carefully consider how we start anything — our inaugural step.

No one is so tall that he need never stretch, and none so small that he need never stoop.

Danish proverb

Don't Underestimate People's Intelligence

Never underestimate people's intelligence! It was the very lesson learnt by a man whose hobby it was to comb the local antique and junk shops of every place he visited. Looking for bargains, his pursuit often proved very lucrative.

Once again, whilst passing through a small town, he spotted such a place. But his expert eye could find nothing of special interest. As he was leaving, he caught sight of a black cat near the door lapping milk from a saucer, which he immediately recognised as a piece of precious china. Convinced that the shop owner, who let his cat use it, could not be aware of its value, he saw an undreamt of opportunity of obtaining a real bargain.

Turning back, he told the dealer that the cat had taken his fancy. It was such a lovely creature that he had fallen for it. 'Will you sell it to me?' he casually asked. And when the owner agreed at once to do so, as if on second thought, the man proposed to take the saucer as well. 'After all, the cat must be used to it and thus won't feel so strange in a new home,' he explained.

'You can have the cat for five dollars, but not the saucer,' the dealer responded. 'You see, I've already sold more than a hundred cats because of that saucer.'

Unexpected Finds

When passing through customs on entering a country, most travellers have nothing to declare. Having picked up their luggage, they proceed quickly along the 'green lane' to join their friends waiting for them or to make their way straight to their destination. But, occasionally, they might be stopped for a 'spot check'. They are then asked to open one or perhaps even all of their cases for inspection.

Therefore, it was really nothing unusual when one of the arriving passengers was asked to open his cases, although he had assured the customs official that he had nothing to declare. In the usual routine, the officer was sliding his hands inside the bag, lifting out several items. Though he was only doing his duty, the traveller resented it. Obviously, the action suggested that he was not being believed.

Giving vent to his annoyance, he turned to the official and, with tongue in cheek, said to him, 'Officer, if you tell me what you are looking for, I'll tell you where you can find it!' Like a flash the man retorted, 'Ah, that's just it. I never know *what* I'm looking for until I've found it!'

Frequently, people ask me how in my research I trace the, at times, most unexpected information. In my reply I recall this story of the customs officer. Many a fascinating 'discovery' I made was not whilst specifically searching for it. I came across it, as it were, by sheer accident. All that is needed is to keep one's eyes and mind open.

This equally applies to your life. There is so much for you to find in exciting discoveries. If only you keep your mind agile and receptive, you will stumble on the most unexpected things, adding special flavour to your life and occupation, no matter what you do and irrespective of your circumstances. These are the hidden opportunities that make life all the richer and more poignant, expanding its horizons and dimensions.

He who seeks will find.

Maori proverb

A Lesson Learnt from Worms

This is the story of a self-made man who made good. He had suffered a serious back injury in a car accident. Unable to work, he went to the country to recuperate. Someone had told him that digging would strengthen his back muscles and accelerate his recovery. So he started to turn over the soil. In the process, he dug up large earthworms.

Struck by their unusual size, and being of an inquiring disposition, his curiosity was roused. Deciding to study them, he embarked on an experiment. Placing some of the worms on a smooth surface, he put others on uneven ground. It did not take long for an interesting change in the worms' behaviour to become apparent. Those on smooth ground became lethargic. There had to be an explanation: because of the monotony of their existence they had lost all former zeal and vigour; it was too flat for them. In contrast, the second group, having to battle and exert themselves, began to thrive.

Our road leads uphill all the way. Without a challenge, we easily become dull and our brains cease to function to full capacity. On the other hand, adversity offers opportunity and the necessity of exertion can serve as a stimulus to success.

Never believe in never.

Avoid Common Errors

Even the most beautifully woven and precious Oriental rug will show some imperfection. This is not the weaver's fault. On the contrary, it is there with a purpose, meant to express the deeply felt religious conviction that nothing created by humans can ever be perfect. Only God is perfect.

Everyone makes mistakes. The most illustrious of people have erred. Even scientists are not exempt. Paradoxically, not a few significant advances were the result of experiments gone wrong. A typical example is the discovery of penicillin.

Greatness is not shown by being faultless. However, it is true wisdom to recognise errors, to set them right and, not least, to avoid making them again. A little consideration could save us and others much heartache, embarrassment and aggravation. It needs little effort to identify some common mistakes and to learn not to make (or repeat) them:

• To judge people by their outward appearance and demeanour, by some merely skin-deep aspect. Our estimation should be based on the intrinsic quality, the character and not the facade.

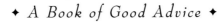

• Not to make allowances for the weakness in others. We are not slow in making excuses for ourselves.

• To downgrade people and, contemptuously, to describe certain of their traits which, if present in ourselves, we would regard meritorious. A typical example of such prejudiced choice of a value-weighted judgment refers to the attitude of persistency. If displayed by ourselves, we praise it as firmness and determination. If shown by others, we condemn it as obstinacy or stubbornness.

• To believe solely in what our limited mind can grasp at present. After all, what may have appeared impossible not so long ago has become an accepted, everyday reality. We live in a world in which the unexpected has become the commonplace.

• Not to yield to insignificant trifles and make an issue of matters that really are unimportant. This would show small-mindedness.

• Not to alleviate a situation which is within our capabilities of remedying, a neglect we might easily come to regret.

• To avoid pulling our weight and to shirk our duty. Some people are like blisters — they never show up until the work has been done! If they only knew how much they miss in not experiencing the thrill of achievement.

All these are common mistakes and none of us is infallible. After all, it is a truism that 'to err is human'. But equally true is what Confucius is alleged to have said, that 'he who has committed an error and does not correct it, is making another mistake'.

Don't Be All-wise

It is so easy to lay down the law and to judge other's situations and circumstances without having experienced them yourself. So many people seem to know best and decry the way those burdened with a problem try to meet it. Be careful not to join their throng.

Be compassionate and sensitive, but never all-wise. Empathy is a precious gift. Like sympathy, it makes us feel and, literally, 'suffer' with the other person. But beware of ever becoming one of those who always know what to do — until it happens to them.

Don't Think it is Just You

You may have had the experience that people with whom you used to be friendly suddenly start to cold-shoulder you or to act strangely towards you. This makes you wonder what it is you may have said to offend them. Have you done anything to hurt them? What is wrong with them, or you, you ask yourself.

You need not worry. Don't think it is merely you whom they treat in this fashion. Most likely, they act peculiarly towards everyone. Hence, don't take it personally. Ask yourself whether these people, being so moody, are worth knowing. If you think they are, just ignore their odd behaviour, or try to talk to them about it. If, on the other hand, you find this to be impossible and you feel that their so-called friendship is too much to take and you are unable to relax with them, simply sever your relationship. Such people are basically unhappy in themselves and therefore cannot be happy for other people.

All you can do is pity such miserable individuals who, for reasons of their own, have turned bitter and ill-natured. If enough people shun them, it may bring them to their senses and make them realise that soon they will have no one left to talk to or to make unhappy which, possibly, will change their attitude.

Do You Know Where You Are Going?

Everyone nowadays seems to be in a hurry and life has become one great mindless rush — to nowhere. People race about, as if every split-second counts. But they don't know where they are going.

A story is told of Thomas H. Huxley, the famous English naturalist, who was scheduled to give a lecture in Dublin. His boat was delayed in docking and he was concerned that this would make him late for his address.

Once disembarked, he jumped into the nearest cab, urging the driver to go at the maximum speed. He then concentrated on the notes he had prepared for his lecture. When, after some time, the taxi had not arrived at the destination, a dreadful thought dawned on Huxley. Turning to the driver, he apprehensively asked, 'Did I tell you where to take me?' 'No, sir,' the cabbie replied, 'but, as you requested, I'm driving as fast as I can.'

It seems so laughable an incident and typical of an absent-minded professor. However, don't many of us follow this very practice in our daily life? Speed is everything, but do we know where we are going? Have

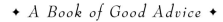

we a definite aim and a plan? Training future
executives, a teacher impressed on them that 'a bad
plan is better than no plan at all'. Very good advice
indeed!

When a man does not know what harbour he is making
for, no wind is the right wind.

Seneca

Make Every Day Count

A good principle to adopt is to make sure that no day
passes without your having learnt something new or
having done something extra. No matter how busy you
might be or how tired, never make an exception. To do
so, you should regard the day as a lost day. Such
practice will enhance your life remarkably and render it
an ongoing adventure and enjoyment. No day will ever
be wasted. On the contrary, thus enriched, it will prove
meaningful, worthwhile and memorable. All you need
to achieve it is willpower.

Don't be Negative

There is both good and bad in the world. Some people primarily notice, or remember, the bad; it strikes their eye at once. If there is a single cloud in the sky or one spot of dirt on the wall, they will immediately see the blemish and forget about the blue sky and the many beautiful things that by far outnumber the blotches.

If you learn to count your blessings and look to the positive side in life, you will make your world all the richer. You yourself will not only be in a much happier frame of mind but make the lives of those you love so much easier and more pleasant. Take every opportunity that offers itself to recognise, and even seek out, the positive. Such gift is an indispensable vitamin for the enjoyment of life. It is a sure cure for the blues.

Nothing is so bad that good can't come from it.
Spanish saying

Don't be sorry that the bottle is half empty. Be glad that it is half full.

Disarming Aggression

A woman driver has a simple way of disarming aggressive male motorists. Responsible and law abiding herself, she takes note of every give-way sign and never tries to cut in front of other cars.

She recalls the many occasions when the driver of the car behind her impatiently honked his horn and then, poking out his head from the window, shouted abuses at her.

She has grown accustomed to a great variety of disparagements. These include such jibes as, 'Where is your learner's plate?', 'You'd better go and get your licence,' or 'Hadn't you better learn to drive!'

It would be so easy on her part to shout back insults. However, cleverly, she has learnt to react in a most unexpected way. Poking out her head in turn, with a smiling face, she will call out, 'You're quite right!'

Her retort never fails to have its desired effect. Mixing metaphors, it takes the wind out of the male driver's sails, cutting short any clash of words. His jaw drops and by the time his mouth closes again, she is well and truly on her way.

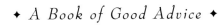

You can silence anger and abuse by not losing your temper. If, in spite of provocation, you remain agreeable, you will disarm all aggressiveness.

If your lips would keep from slips
Five things observe with care:
To whom you speak, of whom you speak,
And how, and when, and where.

I prefer to hear this than to be deaf.

French proverb

In Search of Praise

Constant harping and adverse criticism is abrasive and achieves the opposite of what is intended. Genuine praise (totally different from flattery) on the other hand encourages, and there is not one person who does not appreciate being appreciated. It acts like a spur.

Particularly in a relationship, a couple should never take each other for granted and assume that by now they should know how much they mean to each other. George Eliot's words are so applicable to everyone: 'I like not only to be loved, but to be told that I am loved; the realm of silence is large enough beyond the grave'.

Do you ever tell your partner in so many words how much you love him or her and how greatly you admire the qualities he or she possesses? Do you still show the concern, appreciation and respect, as no doubt you once did in the early days of your courtship or friendship? If not, the omission may be just thoughtlessness on your part. However, it might easily be (mis)interpreted as neglect and loss of interest. This, in turn, might kill any desire on your companion's part to go on trying to please you, thinking, 'Why bother?'

We usually see what we look for. It is so easy to find fault. Never be a negativist, always seeking out the flaws. Doing so will inevitably destroy affection and engender unhappiness. It undoes all the joy of living which could and should be yours and that of those you really love.

Kind words don't wear out the tongue.
Danish proverb

A kind word never got a man into trouble.
Irish saying

Speaking One's Mind

Always say what you mean and mean what you say. There is nothing more stimulating and helpful than to voice one's opinion. This should be done freely and honestly, without hesitation. We must not hold back in being 'outspoken'. However, in whatever we say we should be careful not to offend or hurt those to whom we speak.

True friends will appreciate when, with integrity and honesty, you speak your mind. Those who resent it are not friends. They do not want to hear the truth, at least as you see it. Indeed, they are not even worth knowing.

The naked truth is so much better than the best-dressed lie.

The Curse of Jealousy

Jealousy of any kind is a curse. To be jealous of a person one loves indicates lack of trust. Otherwise, why be jealous? It is not, as sometimes imagined, a sign of love.

La Rochefoucauld so rightly observed that, 'In jealousy there is more self-love than love'. Jealousy has ruined many a happy partnership.

A man who was obsessed by feelings of jealousy constantly looked for signs of his wife's infidelity. If, for instance, she came home from shopping with her lipstick slightly smudged, he would suspect that secretly she had been with another man. No assurances on her part could ever convince him that there was no shred of substance to justify any of his many sick and sickening accusations. Eventually, unable any longer to cope with his attitude, his wife left him. But not for another man. It was because her husband had killed all her love for him.

Whoever harbours such jealous feelings must seek help. They are like a progressive disease. It does not get better with time. On the contrary, it will ultimately assume incurable proportions and poison a relationship.

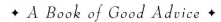

Some people envy others' happiness or success. To suffer such bouts of jealousy is a symptom of their own inadequacy and resentment of another's superiority. Maybe, if they themselves had worked harder, they could have done even better than the one they envy. If you yourself are the victim of jealousy, don't be upset. Take it as the product of unwilling admiration. Paradoxically, you ought even go further and be grateful that people have no reason to pity you.

No one can make you feel inferior without your consent.
Eleanor Roosevelt

What a Smile Can Do

An American couple had just flown into London from the Bahamas. Theirs was a beautiful suntan which certainly made them stand out from all the other people with their pale complexions. Having settled into their hotel, to stretch their legs after sitting for long hours in the plane they decided to go for a walk.

Strolling down Oxford Street, they were stopped by a woman asking directions. Having lived in London for some time, they could easily oblige. It did not take long before someone else approached them and then a third person, with the identical request! This could not be a mere coincidence, they felt. Puzzled, they wondered what it was that made these people choose them to ask for directions, especially as they were not dressed like nor did they look like Londoners.

They decided that, should it recur, they would ask whomever it was why, of all people, he or she had picked them. They did not have to wait long. And after having told their inquirer how to get to the desired destination, they put their question to them. The explanation was most unexpected. 'It's because you have a smile on your face, looking so happy and approachable!'

Indeed, a smile can do so much!

A Smile

A smile costs nothing but gives much —
It takes but a moment, but the memory of it usually lasts
forever.
None are so rich that can get along without it —
And none are so poor but that can be made rich by it.
It enriches those who receive
Without making poor those who give —
It creates sunshine in the home,
Fosters goodwill in business
And is the best antidote for trouble —
And yet it cannot be begged, borrowed or stolen, for it is
of no value
Unless it is freely given away.
Some people are too busy to give you a smile —
Give them one of yours —
For the good Lord knows that no one needs a smile so
badly
As he or she who has no more smiles left to give.

Author unknown

A man without a smile on his face must not open a shop.
Ancient Chinese advice

23

Preserving the Family Unit

A cynic once described a modern home as a 'dormitory over a garage'. Unfortunately, there is much truth in his observation. It is increasingly rare for a family to sit down to a leisurely meal and talk. Mostly, they rush through the food, possibly at the same time looking at television, with conversation being conspicuous by its absence.

Once the meal is over, everyone does his or her own thing. Father might watch a cricket or football match on television, the son retire to his room to play computer games, whilst the daughter is going out on a date, and mother is left to do the dishes. Of course this assumes that the 'children' have not yet moved out of the house.

One family had made it a rule for a night every week to be set aside as 'family night'. There was no exception. Soon it became an accepted and even eagerly awaited practice. Everyone stayed on and, sitting around the dining table, joined in discussing family matters and plans. Jointly they worked out the budget for the ensuing week and each member of the family promised to undertake some specific task.

All were encouraged to freely air their views. Whenever there were differences of opinion, it was agreed to disagree agreeably. It was a family that stayed together, and the children did not move out till they got married and started a home of their own. No doubt, they would carry on the tradition, which they had acquired from their parents as something to be treasured and enjoyed.

Make such a family life your aim.

I am not a Tree

For days on end, a teenager had tried to talk to her father to discuss one of her problems. A business executive, he was always too busy and preoccupied. Rushing off early in the morning, he could not find the time. On his return home late at night, he was too tired to listen.

Whenever she tried to get his attention he put her off, for another time. And even if he found a few moments to spare, she somehow felt that he was not really listening to her or taking her seriously.

So one day she sat down and wrote a poem which she placed at his bedside. He could not miss it and immediately grasped its meaning. Ever since, a new relationship has been established at home. She had taught her father a lesson. He had learnt to listen, to take note.

Her poem, so expressive of the feelings of an anguished child who could not get her parent to listen, is addressed to many a father and mother:

> *Please listen when I speak*
> *I speak for a reason*
> *For people to hear*
> *And for you to listen.*

I speak to be heard
Not to be missed
I like to be spoken to
Not just ignored.

Please listen when I speak
I mean what I say
I don't speak for nothing
I don't speak to play.

Please, I ask
Please listen to me
You may be bored
But think of a tree.

It stands there all day
With nothing to say
Just standing —
I feel that way.

No matter how busy parents are, they must find the time they owe to their children, and do so not casually and spasmodically, but regularly and with a genuine show of concern. Setting aside daily an unhurried period to share with their children, they can make manifold use of it. They can help with the homework or merely play with them. But most of all it should be to listen to their children and their problems. To them these are just as large as yours are to you!

Wrong Legacies

Caring parents feel fulfilled if they have been able to see their children well-established on the road of life. To achieve this aim should be their prime target, but many parents go beyond this. Having reached this important stage, at times at great cost, they continue to deprive themselves. They do so for no other reason than to be able to leave to their children a maximum of worldly goods, to help them along even after their own passing.

Such legacy is based on a fallacy. Once having given the best, and of their best, to their children, they owe it to themselves to live their own lives to the fullest, without giving up anything that may enrich and improve them. Their children now can — and ought to — look after themselves. Just as parents do not want to become a burden to their children, children should not expect gains from their parents, causing them to give up the joys and comforts they so much deserve. Your children will appreciate and value their own achievements all the more. Having things presented to them on a platter is not nearly the same as having to work for, and earn, them.

I put him on the horse — he has to ride.
Hungarian proverb

The Worst Computer Virus

This virus is able to spoil your children's entire future. Its symptom is an addiction to video games. Hooked on this 20th-century toy, it may create an obsession. Children (in the majority it seems to be boys) withdraw into their rooms — and into themselves. All they can think of is getting to their computer, sometimes to sit up with it till late into the night. They become antisocial and taciturn, with their grades at school plummeting.

No one will deny that your children deserve the best. Computers, within reason, can prove a wonderful means of entertainment and education. You may even enhance its value by encouraging your children to use it for learning, rather than merely playing games. You could help or join in, too. But if abused, computers can become harmful. You must take precautionary measures to immunise your children against this virus. Set a limited period each day for play and make sure that the computer is not being touched until all homework is done. Insist and persist, though temporarily you may encounter much opposition and unpleasantness, if not tantrums. In the long run, you will be saved lots of anguish and prevent future failure, stunted intellectual growth and a disturbed psychological equilibrium.

More than enough is too much.

English proverb

We are not Worlds Apart

A Buddhist parable deals with people's arrogant claims to exclusively own the truth and to have the right faith. It tells of a prince who was deeply distressed by the quarrels among his subjects in a district of his realm. Each of them asserted that his views were the correct ones and those of all others false.

The prince was determined to make them realise the foolishness of their attitudes. He asked them to come to his palace and to meet there people who had been born blind. He then brought in an elephant. Speaking to his blind guests, he explained, 'This is an elephant!' He invited each of them to tell him what sort of animal it was. He made some touch the elephant's head. Others were told to feel the tuft of its tail and a third group were asked to embrace one of its legs.

After having made them touch and feel some part of the animal, he asked each person to describe it. Those who had felt its head were sure that an elephant was like a pot. Others who had grasped one of its ears claimed that the creature was like a winnowing basket. 'No! That is totally untrue!' shouted one of those who had taken hold of one of its legs, 'I know for certain that an elephant is like a pillar'.

And so it went on. Each was convinced that his own explanation, based on his fragmentary experience, was the correct one. Eventually, they began to quarrel among themselves, calling each other liars and ignoramuses. Limited in their knowledge, they each nevertheless genuinely believed themselves to be the sole owners of the complete truth.

However different and strange other people's views and convictions seem to us, let us never disparage them, imagining that our own is the superior knowledge and that we have the monopoly of the truth. Truth is like the summit of a mountain none of us has ever reached. We look towards it from our own individual angle. You may do so from one side of the mountain and I from the other. Standing perhaps on opposite slopes, we might appear to be worlds apart. However, in reality, our distance from the peak — the truth — is the same. We only see it from different sides.

If we would only be aware of this partiality of our views, instead of being contentious, we would then learn to appreciate each other's points of view and even in the diversity of our distinctive ways recognise a common aspiration. By combining our various aspects, we would become all the wiser and, jointly, get nearer the truth.

On Being Tolerant

People often pride themselves on their tolerance. But to be tolerant is not enough. Indeed, such self-praise, however unintentional and unrecognised, reflects an attitude of condescension and, metaphorically speaking, could be described as social and religious astigmatism. Almost patronisingly and, as it were, magnanimously, we portray ourselves as 'enduring' and 'bearing' with the other person's views. Little-known is the fact that the word 'tolerance' is derived from a Latin root of that very meaning. Hence, to state 'I am tolerant', literally says 'I bear with you'.

Tolerance thus assumes a superiority of ourselves. Indulgently it looks down on someone of different race, religious conviction, nationality or outlook. After all, nobody can help being what he or she is or does.

Instead of merely being tolerant, we ought to show respect. Everybody has his or her own particular worth in the world, a value which no one can rival. We might not and need not share the other's philosophy of life but that does not justify us to look down on it.

We are what we are — in religion, race, nationality and opinions — not least by circumstances beyond our control, mostly by the accident of our parents and birthplace. Whilst trying to live our own lives to the very best of our ability, according to what seems to us most satisfying and fulfilling, we must allow others to do so as well and duly pay deference to them. Only those who hold convictions respect convictions. As it were, let us live locally but think globally.

The wise man thinks before he speaks.
Samoan proverb

Come to the Point

If you want anything, say so straight out. Don't beat about the bush. Unfortunately, many people think it wise to prepare the ground. They will chatter about all kinds of things, but the real reason for their call.

A discerning observer discovered a definite routine in such conversation. Like a classical symphony, it consisted of four movements. The weather formed the first topic: how warm or cold, dry or wet, or unseasonable it has been. This meteorological discussion was followed by a brief review of the political scene. Next in line were common acquaintances. And only then, as the fourth movement, at long last, came mention of the actual subject in mind.

Though the sequence of the first movements and their extent may vary, the conclusion is always the primary cause of the call, giving insignificance to everything that has previously been said. Oddly, you will also find that usually in such an approach the real objective, once arrived at, is often introduced by the clause,
'Oh, by the way . . .'

Avoid such artificial overtures which make your entire conversation phoney. Come to the point at once. Leave for last any pleasantries, and keep them to the absolute minimum. Your request will be all the more effective and will be listened to if you put it first.

Table Talk

A large family met at regular intervals for dinner and only the most urgent circumstances would be accepted as an excuse for staying away. There were always some invited guests. Altogether, it was not the usual kind of dinner.

First of all, on each occasion the seats were thoughtfully assigned. You never had the same table partners. More significant was the unique handwritten menu placed in front of everyone. This not only listed the individual dishes to be served but specified next to each course a topic you were expected to discuss with your neighbour whilst partaking of it, and during the purposely lengthy intervals that followed prior to the next course. It was to give you ample time to digest the indicated subject matters in depth.

When departing, everyone had not only enjoyed the meal but had been enriched and stimulated with much food for thought. It was a well-planned exchange of ideas on a great variety of themes, indeed, a memorable get-together.

We have lost this art of conversation. Would it not be something truly exhilarating and mentally nourishing to make at least some of our meals occasions of such 'table talk'?

When Time Seems to Drag

Frequently people complain that time hangs heavy on their hands. They say, 'I've nothing to look forward to. Every day is the same. I dread waking up in the morning as I don't know what to do with myself for the rest of the day.'

On the other hand, there are those who complain that time passes too quickly, regretfully asking, 'Where have the years gone?' If they only realized how lucky they are. Theirs was the blessing of the fullness of life.

Everyone should (and can) fill the day with something that provides satisfaction and a feeling of achievement. Not least so those who have retired or lack a regular occupation or employment. A multitude of tasks awaits them. Somewhere — particularly so in service to the community — there is a need and a niche for everyone. All you have to do is to find it.

You can help others not as fortunate as yourself. It will give a new meaning to your life and much happiness. Your time will be taken up with lots to do and, in the process, you will meet others in a similar position who, in turn, will be happy to have your company. This way, too, you will be able to plan your days ahead. Never bored, you will look forward to all that is to come.

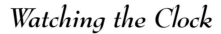

Watching the Clock

Some people have a very bad habit. Whilst talking to others, without even realising it, they look at their watch. They do so not merely once, but repeatedly. They are not only unaware of it but would not even be able to say what time it was. Unfortunately, however, this idiosyncrasy might easily be misinterpreted as the desire to terminate the conversation.

It makes so feasible the advice once given to American businesspeople who were about to discuss possible contracts with an Eastern nation. Not to appear impatient, they were asked to take off their watches prior to meeting their potential client.

A small philosophical society which always met in private homes had adopted a very thoughtful custom. After having introduced its speaker, the host conspicuously turned the clock on the mantelpiece around so that its face could not be seen. It was a beautiful gesture to show that no one should be concerned with the mechanical passage of time now that their minds were about to focus on timeless thought.

You need your watch. But don't become its slave, chasing the hours.

We can alter our lives by altering our attitudes.
William James

Be on Time

General Sir John Monash, renowned as a great Australian figure both in war and peace, was a stickler for punctuality. To be 'according to schedule' became almost an obsession. He made it his principle always to arrive 'on the dot'. Should the car taking him to his appointment be too early, he would ask his chauffeur to drive around the block, if necessary several times, to arrive at exactly the stipulated hour. On other occasions, he would get out of the car and go for a short walk, to return 'just on time'.

A diversity of reasons makes people late. Some thoughtless individuals just do not care whether they keep others waiting. Others, ego-driven, deliberately go out of their way to be late. They want to be noticed and, as it were, to be waited for. They consider it a sign of superiority not to appear overanxious to be present, easily achieved by being conspicuously late. Their delay would also indicate how busy and in demand they were, hardly able to spare the time.

Many meetings and functions do not start at the advertised hour. Frequently, the reason given for the delay is that a certain party has not yet arrived. This penalises those considerate enough to make sure not to be late. Unpunctuality, without a valid and significant reason, shows lack of respect. It is not merely discourteous but insulting. To have been held up in heavy traffic is a poor excuse. Such eventuality can often be anticipated, enabling one to leave home in good time.

To be on time not only expresses courtesy and thoughtfulness, but it is a habit that makes us usefully employ every moment of life. I can truthfully say that the only time I have ever wasted was being 'on time'.

Courtesy pleases much and costs little.
Chinese saying

A Useful Reminder

There is a strange paradox in the American way of life. To most Americans time is money and they have learnt to apply the principle wherever possible. This has made them excel in time and motion study.

Though anxious to save every precious minute, when it comes to their meals, cumulatively they waste many hours. Americans cut up their food first. They then put down the knife, change the fork from the left to their right hand, and at last begin eating. Inevitably, this procedure prolongs the time spent on their meals.

At a dinner party in Los Angeles an English guest was surprised to notice one of the Americans eating the non-American way. It so happened that just prior to sitting down to the meal this very man, a well-known industrialist, had told him of being a third generation American. As he seemed an approachable kind of person, the Englishman did not hesitate to ask him for an explanation.

The American did not resent it at all. 'I'm pleased you asked me about it,' he said. He had come from a large family who had had to struggle hard to make ends meet. Many a time there was not sufficient food to go round. Through a mere accident, he became aware that if he ate the European way he was so much faster, with the result that he was able to finish his meal before all the others. If any second helpings were left, they were his! Thus it became his habit to eat the non-American way. 'I can honestly say,' he continued, 'that I'm happy about it, as it reminds me constantly of those early days when I was poor, and how grateful I should be for my good fortune.'

Many achievers forget their humble beginnings. Once having 'arrived', ego-driven, they become uncaring. Never deny your past nor become a snobbish upstart. Show gratitude for your success by remaining humble and seeking out those less fortunate, to support and foster them.

A man learns little from victory but much from defeat.
Japanese saying

Self-destructing Problems

You may have experienced how, during the hours of darkness, a little worry becomes magnified. Lying in bed wide awake, you think of all the things that might happen — though mostly they never do. This is no consolation when you cannot sleep. Many a sleepless night is the result of trivial things taking on tremendous proportions.

A similar common problem relates to some unfinished task. Generally, people believe that 'sleeping on it' will clarify their mind and, refreshed next morning, what seemed an insurmountable obstacle will be easily tackled. Maybe unconsciously, they resolve it during their sleep. Though this might work for some, the majority of people are not so fortunate. They cannot go to bed without first having confronted the issue. In the case of an important letter, for instance, they will sit down and draft it, even if only roughly, well realising that the next day they might have to change it altogether. At least they get it out of their system and can lie down and go to sleep without writing and rewriting it in their mind — time and time again — in the darkness of the bedroom.

A man had adopted a strange method in dealing with troublesome problems that threatened to destroy his peace of mind. He did not dwell on them, however, when they occurred, he wrote them on a piece of paper which he put into a large vase. This he routinely emptied at the end of each month to discover that many of the problems he had noted down had solved themselves!

Worry, indeed, is a poison which can manacle your mind and play havoc with your health. As the saying goes, 'it is not what you eat that gives you ulcers but what is eating you'. In addition, it will make those near to you tense as well because, being so close to you, they can sense your uneasiness and suffer from your edginess. Learn to deal with your problems or put them into 'cold storage'. In the majority of cases they will be self-destructing. Thus you not only get a good night's rest but will be spared moods of depression and clouds of doubt. You will discover within yourself an enormous store of staying power and resilience. In Tennyson's words, 'strong in will', you will be able 'to strive, to seek, to find and not to yield'.

Don't burn up your blanket to get rid of a flea.
Turkish proverb

The Friendship Quilt

In the Deep South of the United States of America, colourful quilts are part of many an antebellum home. They were made up of numerous squares of different materials, though of the same size. Some were embroidered and others had names or initials stitched on them.

They were known as 'friendship quilts'. And for a very valid reason. Through the years, a housewife would collect bits and pieces of material. She then distributed these among her friends, who made them into squares of their own design. Sewn together, they created the friendship quilt. Apart from being decorative, it served as a bedspread and gave warmth on cold winter nights.

Today some of these friendship quilts are treasured as priceless possessions and meaningful heirlooms. Most of all, they are a constant reminder of the value of friendship — it adds warmth and beauty to life.

Few things are worse than being lonely. We all need friends, real friends, not merely friendly people. True friendship is priceless and can never be bought. It is in times of adversity that one discovers who one's real friends are. Those who desert you and no longer want to know you were only fair-weather acquaintances. In the words of Walter Winchell, the renowned American journalist and broadcaster, 'A real friend is one who walks in when the rest of the world walks out.' When young, we want to have friends. When old, it is essential to have a friend. But to have a friend, we must be a friend.

The richest man is not the one who still has the first dollar he ever earned, but it is the man who still has his first friend.

The Lace Handkerchief

People often wrongly quote the Bible as stating that 'money is the root of all evil'. This is incorrect. It refers not to money, but to the *love* of money. The passage speaks of those who are obsessed with money and lack social responsibility, imagining that wealth is the be-all and end-all of their lives, bestowing on them a special status. Money in itself is neutral. It can be good or bad. Indeed, if properly used, it may prove beneficial, providing help and greatly enhancing people's existence.

Some successful entrepreneurs share a conspicuous feature. After having amassed a fortune, they go on making money; the first million no longer satisfies them. Do such people not realise that what counts most in life are the things that cannot be counted?

An American woman who belonged to this 'lucky' class of millionaires was discussing this very question with an acquaintance who did not hold back in voicing, politely but firmly, their opinion of some people's over-estimation of wealth and how tragic life could be when one had plenty to live on and nothing to live for.

The woman listened quietly and then gave her reply which was personal and very much to the point. 'If I have to cry,' she said, 'I prefer to cry into a lace handkerchief.' However, she also agreed that the good life means the good uses of life!

A Confusion of Values

Desperate parents frequently ask, 'Where did we go wrong with our children that they have turned out the opposite to what we had hoped?' They had given them everything — all the things they did not have when growing up themselves.

That, precisely, is the explanation. Many modern parents overindulge their children, giving them too much too soon. Because they had to struggle to obtain the things they needed, they want to spare their children this hardship.

They do not realise the advantage they have had by having had to battle. Because they were brought up frugally, when they fell on hard times, they knew how to economise and to do the most with the least, effectively and efficiently; they stayed afloat.

Another essential consideration in bringing up children is to set them an example in family stability and intrinsic values — both morally and ethically. The proper way to live is not taught, but caught.

Don't be a Successful Failure

Everyone admires success. It is a more than common saying that, 'nothing succeeds like success'. Stories of rags to riches, told in one form or another, have always been popular. The newsboy or shoeshine who rose to the position of industrial executive, bank president or millionaire entrepreneur is merely the twentieth-century version of Cinderella.

Do we know what success really means? Many imagine that to be successful is to amass a fortune, to live in a luxurious home and drive a large, powerful car, to gain prominence and fame and become what psychologists have called an 'overachiever'.

To attain this aim, many people are prepared to sacrifice everything of real value: their family life, ethical standards, and even their health. They mistake power and wealth for happiness. Such spurious success has ruined many a life and explains why this world is so full of successful failures.

A social historian gave a vivid example which, though now belonging to the past, is still very applicable to the present. He recalls a gathering in 1923 in a Chicago hotel of some of the world's then most 'successful' men. No doubt, at the time, they were the envy of many. Among them was the president of the largest industrial complex, a brilliant figure of the wheat market, a member of the American cabinet, and Ivar Kreuger, the 'match king', whose dream it was to control the production of matches worldwide and who already owned factories in 34 countries.

Checking on their fate 25 years later, their lives told a different story. One of the men had died penniless, another was serving a prison sentence, and Ivar Kreuger had committed suicide. Like most high-flyers, all these men might have known how to make a fabulous living, but none of them knew how to *live*. Success is not anything material, you cannot buy happiness. Indeed, it has often been proved that 'less is more'.

A Built-in Safety Valve

When angry, people react differently. Some will flare up and, with a raised voice, give vent to their feelings. But having done so the air is cleared, like after a thunderstorm, and they will forget all about it.

Those of the opposite disposition will show no reaction — outwardly. They will eat it all in. Worse still, going to the other extreme, for days on end they will not speak at all to whomever they blame for having caused the clash. Shutting up like a clam, they will go on to brood about the (often imagined) insult.

There is no doubt which of the two temperaments is the healthier. Those who externalise their anger might temporarily raise their blood pressure, but once the storm is passed, they will bear no grudge or resentment. The second type, however, will harbour the hurt, which will go on rankling inside. With nothing being solved or resolved, they will be worse off in the end, possibly getting ulcers or harming their health in other ways.

A couple who were about to celebrate an important anniversary of their truly happy union recalled an incident early in their marriage. At the time they had had a terrible row, with the result that the husband stormed out of the house, in the process slamming the door so hard that it broke. Twenty years later, neither of them could even remember what the disagreement had been about.

Do What You Can — When You Can

There are many people who hesitate. They could be called the 'not yets' who, when called upon to do anything, no matter whether for their family, the community, or their country, like to wait. They always want to postpone things: till their children are older, their position more secure, or they themselves more ready. Only then do they intend to join in, contribute or participate. They should remember that in life it is principally the undertaker who makes the final arrangements. Even a little too late is much too late.

We need 'instant' people, those who live with confidence and are prepared to act now!

One of those days is none of these days.

English proverb

I've Had It!

'I've had it!' So short a phrase, it has become a common outcry of utter frustration.

In worrisome times of economic problems, unemployment, bankruptcy and the splitting up of families, often as a result of those very conditions, one hears more and more people use it. They begin to lose heart and weariness accompanies them wherever they go.

Nothing can be more demoralising than being idle. No one can endure the horror of inaction for long. Inevitably, the mind becomes sluggish. However, anyone can change the problem into a challenge. Even in the worst of crises, no one need be out of work. Incredible is the multiplicity of possible tasks awaiting those who want to stay active and employed. There are always cars to be washed, lawns to be mown, fences to be mended, homes to be cleaned, children to be minded and the elderly to be helped with day-to-day tasks which have become too much for them. All that is necessary is initiative, imagination and flexibility.

No job is degrading, as the fulfilment of any function, if done conscientiously and with enthusiasm, will bring its reward. You will get the best out of others if you give the best of yourself. Whatever you work at will work for you. It will give you self-respect and gain you appreciation.

As an unexpected bonus in such pursuit, new avenues will suddenly open up and novel interests will be generated. It is not the position that gives prestige to the person who occupies it, but the individual who bestows responsibility to the task he or she undertakes — any task! 'Keep your face to the sun and the shadows will fall behind'. Above all, remember that happiness does not depend upon events, and realise that life is larger than today's problems. An enterprising person is always capable of working his way upward.

Whoever cares to learn will always find a teacher.
German proverb

What One Person Can Do

The defeatist says that one person alone can do nothing. However, it is one person, one single individual, who can do anything. The best advice, when you need it most, always comes from one person.

One human being can do so much evil and also so much good. History has shown many an example. One person with courage, it has so rightly been said, makes a majority. Of course, it all depends on the type of person.

Three examples may serve as an illustration of the lasting effect of an individual's action extending over a wide range of spheres.

A man was standing at the curbside in a small American city, waiting for the bus to take him to his office. Looking down, he saw a piece of wire lying in the gutter. He picked it up and started playfully twisting it around one of his fingers. While doing so, the idea suddenly came to him that, if properly bent, such wire could prove most useful in holding together loose sheets of paper. Then and there, he invented the paperclip, starting a multi-million dollar industry! What *one* person can do with imagination!

That the superstition about spilling salt was adopted almost universally is due to one man as well — Leonardo da Vinci. In his painting *The Last Supper,* he depicted an overturned saltcellar in front of Judas. The Last Supper preceded the crucifixion and Judas is said to have betrayed his master. The spilling of salt in front of him was meant to express his close link with the imminent misfortune. And as Leonardo's painting became world famous, the superstition was spread far and wide. What *one* person can do — by attention to detail!

One of the guests at a society wedding in New York, held towards the end of last century, had come all the way from England. On his way to the church he was caught in a thunderstorm. Being immaculately dressed, he did not want to get the bottoms of his trousers wet and dirty and, for this reason, slightly rolled them up. However, being in a hurry, he forgot to turn them back before entering the church. The large number of spectators who, in spite of the storm and rain, had gathered to watch all the celebrities arrive, could not help but notice the strange attire of the Englishman when he was ascending the steps.

They imagined this to be the latest London fashion (then the trendsetter) and subsequently asked their tailors to copy it. Thus, cuffs or turn-ups on trousers came into existence, to be adopted by men all over the world. What *one* person can do inadvertently — by forgetfulness!

A little girl refused to go to sleep unless the door of her room was left open. One day her mother asked her the reason, 'Do you want the door kept open to let in the light?' 'No, Mummy,' the child replied, 'to let out the dark.' And we can let out the dark from many people's lives by realising what *one* person can do by imagination, attention to detail, determination and even inadvertently.

People don't fail because they give up trying. The trouble is too many of us stop trying in trying times. Surely, as a psychiatrist explained, 'It is easier to lie on a couch, digging up the past, than it is to sit on a chair facing up to the present.' It is even harder to get up and walk towards the future to make it a happy reality. You can do so by remembering what *one* person can do. And you could be such a person!

Without going you can get nowhere.
Chinese proverb